SAGITTARIUS:

A COMPLETE GUIDE TO THE SAGITTARIUS ASTROLOGY STAR SIGN

Sofia Visconti

Contents

INTRODUCTION

Astrology has intrigued humans for centuries. It is a practice that involves interpreting the positions and movements of bodies like planets and stars to gain understanding about human experiences. Astrologers analyze the positions of the sun, moon, planets and other celestial bodies within a belt in the sky known as the zodiac. This belt is divided into twelve signs that are associated with human characteristics and qualities. In this book we embark on a journey to explore the world of astrology in depth with a focus on the Sagittarius zodiac sign.

The main goal of this book is to provide an exploration of the Sagittarius zodiac sign. Sagittarius, symbolized by the archer, is renowned for its curiosity and optimistic outlook. However there's more to this sign than meets the eye. We'll delve into the history and mythology surrounding Sagittarius to uncover tales and symbolic representations that have shaped its character. Throughout the book readers will come across insights and practical advice on how to harness Sagittarius strengths effectively while navigating any challenges.

Come along on a journey that unravels the secrets of Sagittarius and reveals the insights that astrology holds.

SAGITTARIUS ZODIAC SIGN OVERVIEW AND SYMBOLISM

- **Date of Star Sign**: Sagittarius falls between November 22nd and December 21st. It is the ninth sign of the zodiac.
- **Symbol**: The symbol of Sagittarius is the Archer. This is often depicted as a centaur (half-human, half-horse) drawing a bow and arrow. This symbol embodies the adventurous and dynamic nature of this sign.
- **Element**: Sagittarius belongs to the Fire element. Fire signs are known for their passion, energy and enthusiasm. Sagittarians are no exception. They exhibit fiery qualities in various aspects of their lives.
- **Planet**: The ruling planet of Sagittarius is Jupiter which is the largest planet in our solar system. Jupiter represents expansion, growth and the

search for knowledge. It amplifies the Sagittarian traits of optimism and exploration.

- **Color**: The color associated with Sagittarius is deep blue or purple. These symbolize wisdom, depth and spirituality. Such colors resonate with the philosophical and adventurous nature of Sagittarius.

COMPATIBILITY

Sagittarius tends to have high compatibility, with Fire signs like Aries and Leo. They also connect well with Air signs such as Gemini, Libra and Aquarius. These signs share a zest for life and intellectual pursuits. However they might face challenges in their relationships with Earth signs like Taurus, Virgo and Capricorn. In addition, Water signs like Cancer, Scorpio and Pisces may clash due to differences in temperament and priorities. Nonetheless with patience and understanding Sagittarius can connect meaningfully with any sign.

PERSONALITY TRAITS

Sagittarius individuals are characterized by a range of distinctive personality traits.

- **Optimistic**: Sagittarians are eternal optimists. They are always looking on the bright side of life. As such they have an infectious enthusiasm that uplifts those around them.
- **Adventurous**: They have an insatiable desire for adventure and exploration. They love to travel,

learn about different cultures and embrace new experiences.

- **Independent**: Independence is highly valued by Sagittarius. They are self-reliant. Freedom and autonomy is valuable to them.
- **Philosophical**: Sagittarians are often drawn to philosophy, spirituality and higher learning. They seek meaning in life and are on a constant quest for knowledge.
- **Honest**: Honesty is a key trait of Sagittarius individuals. They value truthfulness and speak their minds. Sometimes bluntly.
- **Generous**: Sagittarians are generous by nature, always willing to lend a helping hand or share with others.

STRENGTHS

Sagittarius individuals possess several strengths, including:

- **Open-Mindedness**: They are open to new ideas and perspectives.
- **Problem solvers;** Overall they are excellent problem solvers.
- **Courage**: Sagittarians have the bravery to pursue their goals and take on challenges.
- **Sense of Humor**: They have a great sense of humor and can find laughter even in difficult situations.
- **Intelligence**: Sagittarius individuals are often highly intelligent and quick learners.

- **Adaptability**: They are adaptable and can thrive in various environments.

WEAKNESSES

While Sagittarius has many positive traits, they also have some weaknesses:

- **Impulsivity**: Their adventurous spirit can lead to impulsive decisions and actions.
- **Restlessness**: Sagittarius may struggle with commitment and become restless if they feel tied down.
- **Bluntness**: Their honesty can sometimes come across as tactlessness or insensitivity.
- **Overconfidence**: Their optimism can lead to overconfidence and taking on too much.

In the opening chapter of our exploration into the Sagittarius zodiac sign we have set forth on a journey into astrology. We have introduced you to the qualities and symbols that define Sagittarius. From its Archer symbol to its association with the fiery element of Fire and its governance by Jupiter. Moreover we delved into the influence of blue and purple, the colors that resonate with Sagittarius' adventurous spirit and philosophical nature.

As you delve deeper into the pages of this book you can expect an exploration of Sagittarius history and mythology. We will uncover tales and symbols that have influenced Sagittariuss character over time. Our journey will take us through the tapestry of Sagittarius personality providing insights and practical advice on how to embrace their strengths and navigate potential challenges. You'll also gain an understanding of how Sagittarius individuals approach love, career and much more. Furthermore we will offer an overview of astrological concepts and terminology to ensure that you can fully grasp the complexities of the zodiac.

Whether you're new to astrology or an experienced enthusiast, this book is designed to be a resource for self discovery, personal development and forging a connection with the celestial forces that shape our lives. So as we embark on this journey together by turning the page, prepare yourself to unravel the mysteries surrounding Sagittarius and tap into the wisdom bestowed upon us by astrology. Prepare yourself to delve into the realm of the Archer with an open mind and a sense of adventure as we embark on a journey to uncover the cosmos of the Sagittarius zodiac sign.

CHAPTER 1:
HISTORY AND MYTHOLOGY

elcome to a captivating journey, into the history and mythology of the Sagittarius zodiac sign. In this chapter we will uncover tales, cultural interpretations and enduring legacies that have shaped the archer we recognize today. From the earliest observations of the Sagittarius constellation to its modern significance in astrology. Here we will traverse through time exploring how this symbol has captivated human imagination. As we unveil narratives and historical events that unfolded during Sagittarius season we'll gain insights into how this sign has profoundly influenced history and our understanding of cosmic forces that shape our existence. So come along as we step into the realm of Sagittarius, a place where myths intertwine with history.

HISTORICAL & MYTHOLOGICAL ORIGINS

The constellation Sagittarius, often referred to as "The Archer" or "The Centaur," has a rich history that spans numerous ancient civilizations. In the night sky it has been a prominent feature for thousands of years. Its interpretations and representations have varied among different cultures.

BABYLONIAN AND SUMERIAN CIVILIZATIONS

The earliest known observations and records of the Sagittarius constellation can be traced back to the ancient Babylonians and Sumerians. They associated this constellation with the god Nergal. This deity was often depicted as a centaur-like figure holding a bow and arrow. Nergal was linked to war and the scorching heat of the sun. Such traits align with the symbolism of the Archer.

GREEK AND ROMAN MYTHOLOGY

In Greek mythology, Sagittarius is associated with the centaur, Chiron. A wise healer and mentor to various heroes, including Achilles and Hercules. Chiron was accidentally wounded by a poisoned arrow. This led to his transformation into the constellation. The Greeks and Romans adapted this mythological figure into the centaur archer, depicted with a bow and arrow.

INDIAN ASTRONOMY (VEDIC ASTROLOGY)

In Indian astronomy, Sagittarius is associated with the nakshatra (lunar mansion) called Mula, which means "The Root." It is symbolized by a bunch of roots or a tied bunch of roots. These represent the origins and foundational aspects of life. This cultural interpretation ties into the Archer's role as a seeker of deeper truths and wisdom.

ARABIAN AND ISLAMIC ASTRONOMY

In medieval Islamic astronomy, Sagittarius was known as "Qaws al-Sa'd," which translates to "The Arrow of the Archer." Islamic scholars preserved and expanded upon the knowledge of the Greek and Roman constellations, including Sagittarius, during the Middle Ages.

CHINESE CONSTELLATIONS

Chinese astronomy had its own constellations and celestial maps, separate from the Western zodiac. The concept of Sagittarius does not have a direct equivalent in traditional Chinese astronomy. However, some Chinese star maps and cosmological texts mention Western constellations like Sagittarius due to cultural exchanges over the centuries.

Overall, the Sagittarius constellation has played a significant role in the mythologies and early astronomical observations of diverse ancient civilizations. Its representation as an archer or centaur has been a recurring theme, reflecting humanity's fascination with the celestial wonders above and the stories we tell to make sense of them. These historical and mythological origins have left an indelible mark on our understanding of the Sagittarius zodiac sign and continue to shape our appreciation of this constellation today.

With advancements in astronomy and astrology there has been a refinement in our understanding of the zodiac. New Age concepts have gained popularity in astrology. These explore metaphysical aspects of the zodiac. Astrology is now viewed as a tool for self awareness, personal growth and spiritual development.

HISTORICAL EVENTS UNDER THE SAGITTARIUS SEASON

Throughout history, the astrological season of Sagittarius, has witnessed numerous important events with potential astrological significance. These events often reflect the characteristics and themes associated with the Sagittarius zodiac sign. Namely, exploration, adventure, and philosophical pursuits. Below are some notable historical events that have taken place during the Sagittarius season.

- Ferdinand Magellan's circumnavigation of the globe (1519-1522) and the Apollo 17 moon landing (1972) occurred during this time. Both reflect Sagittarius' adventurous spirit.

- Philosophical and Ideological Shifts: The publication of Charles Darwin's "On the Origin of Species" (1859) and the Wright brothers' first powered flight (1903) marked significant moments of intellectual and technological advancement. Both align with Sagittarius' quest for knowledge and progress.

- Historical Declarations: The United Nations Universal Declaration of Human Rights was adopted on December 10, 1948. Both emphasize ideals of justice, equality and global cooperation associated with this sign.

HISTORICAL FIGURES BORN UNDER THE SAGITTARIUS SIGN

Several influential historical figures have been born under the Sagittarius sign. They embody its traits and have left a lasting impact on history. Notable Sagittarius-born figures include:

- **Winston Churchill:** Born on November 30, 1874, Churchill's leadership during World War II and his gift for oratory align with Sagittarius' characteristics of courage, optimism and communication.

- **Mark Twain:** Samuel Clemens, known as Mark Twain, born on November 30, 1835, epitomized Sagittarius' humor, wit and adventurous storytelling through his classic works like "The Adventures of Tom Sawyer" and "The Adventures of Huckleberry Finn."
- **Frank Sinatra:** The legendary singer and entertainer, born on December 12, 1915, showcased Sagittarius' love for music, performance, and a larger-than-life persona.

From its earliest origins to its modern significance in astrology, Sagittarius has remained a captivating emblem of exploration, adventure and the pursuit of deeper understanding. As we navigate through the changing realm of astrology, Sagittarius serves as a timeless reminder of the fundamental attributes that define our human essence. It urges us to embrace our adventurous side, to seek answers, beyond knowledge and to continuously explore the depths of our own inner selves.

FURTHER READING AND REFERENCES

For readers who wish to delve deeper into the history and mythology of Sagittarius, here is a list of primary sources, ancient texts and modern writings that provide valuable insights into this captivating sign.

- "Enuma Anu Enlil" - An ancient Babylonian cuneiform tablet containing references to Nergal, associated with Sagittarius.

- "Metamorphoses" by Ovid - A classical Roman poem that features the story of Chiron, the centaur associated with Sagittarius.

- "The Mahabharata" - An ancient Indian epic that explores philosophical and mythological themes, relevant to Sagittarius' symbolism.

- "The Only Astrology Book You'll Ever Need" by Joanna Martine Woolfolk - A comprehensive guide to astrology that includes insights on Sagittarius and other zodiac signs.

- "The Secret Language of Birthdays" by Gary Goldschneider and Joost Elffers - Provides personality profiles for each day of the year, offering a unique perspective on Sagittarius individuals.

- "Astrology for the Soul" by Jan Spiller - Focuses on the soul's evolutionary journey through the zodiac signs, including Sagittarius.

CHAPTER 2:
LOVE & COMPATIBILITY

Step into the enchanting world of love and compatibility where we explore the realm of Sagittarius. In this section we will dive into the realm of romance and relationships through the unique perspective of Sagittarius. Sagittarius is renowned for its love, for freedom, exploration and boundless enthusiasm infusing an energy into matters of the heart. Within these pages we will uncover the approach that Sagittarius takes towards love and how it harmonizes with zodiac signs. Whether you are a Sagittarius seeking insights into your love life or simply curious about this sign this chapter guarantees to illuminate the intricacies of a Sagittarians journey.

Sagittarius individuals bring their unique blend of enthusiasm, optimism and adventure into their romantic lives. They are known for their free-spirited nature and love of exploration. Naturally this extends to their relationships. Here's a closer look at Sagittarius' approach to love:

- **Freedom and Independence**: Sagittarians value their freedom and independence highly. They are not ones to be tied down or constrained by possessiveness. In relationships, they seek partners who understand and respect their need for personal space and autonomy.

- **Optimism and Positivity**: Sagittarius individuals radiate positivity. This makes them attractive and enjoyable to be around. They approach love with a hopeful and open heart. Always believing in the best outcomes.

- **Adventurous Spirit**: Just as in other aspects of life, Sagittarians bring their adventurous spirit into their romantic relationships. They love trying new things. For example going on spontaneous trips and exploring together. They thrive on the excitement of shared experiences.

- **Honesty and Bluntness**: Sagittarians are known for their honesty. Sometimes to the point of bluntness. They appreciate partners who can handle their directness. In return they value straightforward communication.

- **Commitment-Phobia**: While Sagittarius individuals may appear commitment-phobic due to their love of freedom. They are not incapable of forming deep and committed relationships. When they do commit, it's because they genuinely value and love their partner. They simply need a partner who understands their need for occasional space and adventure.

- **Intellectual Stimulation**: Sagittarius individuals are intellectually curious. As such they appreciate partners who can engage them in meaningful conversations. Ones who share their love for learning and exploring new ideas.

- **Challenges of Routine**: The routine and predictability of day-to-day life can sometimes become a challenge for Sagittarius in a long-term relationship. They need partners who can inject spontaneity and excitement into their lives to keep the spark alive.

- **Generosity**: Sagittarians are generous by nature. They often go out of their way to make their partners feel loved and cherished. As such they may surprise their loved ones with thoughtful gestures and gifts.

- **Non-Judgmental**: Sagittarius individuals are open-minded and non-judgmental when it comes to love. They are accepting of different backgrounds, cultures and lifestyles. Overall this makes it easier for them to connect with a diverse range of people.

In summary, Sagittarius' approach to love and romance is characterized by their love of freedom, optimism and adventurous spirit. While they may seem commitment-averse at times. They are fully capable of forming deep, meaningful relationships with partners who understand and appreciate their need for independence and exploration.

SAGITTARIUS COMPATIBILITY WITH OTHER ZODIAC SIGNS

Sagittarius, the adventurous and optimistic Archer of the zodiac, approaches love with an open heart and a sense of excitement. They are enthusiastic, independent and always up for new experiences. Let's explore how Sagittarius' love and compatibility play out with each of the other zodiac signs.

SAGITTARIUS AND ARIES

Aries and Sagittarius share a strong connection due to their shared element, Fire. They both crave adventure, spontaneity and a lively relationship. Their shared enthusiasm and love for action creates a passionate and fun-loving bond. However both can be impulsive and headstrong. This may lead to occasional conflicts. However, their shared zest for life usually helps them to overcome disagreements.

SAGITTARIUS AND TAURUS

Taurus' practicality and stability may clash with Sagittarius' love for freedom and adventure. These differences can create challenges in the relationship. Meanwhile Sagittarius can add excitement to Taurus' life.

Sagittarius may find Taurus too possessive. Taurus may see Sagittarius as unreliable or restless. If they can find common ground, Taurus can provide a sense of security to Sagittarius.

SAGITTARIUS AND GEMINI

This is a harmonious pairing. Both signs are curious, adaptable and love communication. Commitment may be an issue for Sagittarius, who can be seen as commitment-phobic by Gemini, who values consistency in a relationship. However, their shared love for exploration and learning creates a dynamic and playful relationship.

SAGITTARIUS AND CANCER

Cancer's emotional depth can clash with Sagittarius' need for independence and adventure, creating potential conflicts. Cancer's desire for stability may seem stifling to Sagittarius, while Sagittarius' restlessness may cause insecurity in Cancer. If both partners are willing to compromise, Cancer can provide emotional support. Sagittarius can introduce Cancer to exciting experiences.

SAGITTARIUS AND LEO

This is a dynamic and passionate match, as both signs share the Fire element. They admire each other's confidence and love for excitement. Their shared enthusiasm and adventurous spirit create a strong and passionate connection. Both can be stubborn and desire to be the leader, leading to power struggles. However, their mutual respect usually helps resolve conflicts.

SAGITTARIUS AND VIRGO

Virgo's practicality and attention to detail may clash with Sagittarius' free-spirited nature, creating challenges in the relationship. Virgo's need for routine may frustrate Sagittarius, who values freedom and adventure. If they can appreciate each other's differences, Virgo can provide stability and structures. Sagittarius can introduce excitement and spontaneity.

SAGITTARIUS AND LIBRA

Libra's social nature and Sagittarius' love for exploration create a harmonious and intellectually stimulating partnership. Although Sagittarius' bluntness and directness may occasionally hurt Libra's sensitive feelings. Ultimately they share a passion for culture, travel, and socializing, making for a vibrant and lively relationship.

SAGITTARIUS AND SCORPIO

This pairing may face challenges due to their differing emotional needs and communication styles. Sagittarius' need for freedom may trigger Scorpio's jealousy and possessiveness. If they can build trust and open up to each other, Scorpio can offer emotional depth and intensity. Sagittarius can bring excitement and optimism.

SAGITTARIUS AND SAGITTARIUS

When two Sagittarians come together, they share a mutual love for adventure, travel and exploration. Their shared interests and enthusiasm create a dynamic, fun-loving relationship full of exciting experiences. Both may struggle with commitment and routine, as they value their independence. However, they understand each other's need for freedom.

SAGITTARIUS AND CAPRICORN

This pairing may face challenges due to their differing priorities and approaches to life. Capricorn can provide stability and structure to Sagittarius, while Sagittarius can introduce Capricorn to spontaneity and fun. Sagittarius may see Capricorn as too serious and traditional, while Capricorn may find Sagittarius unreliable.

SAGITTARIUS AND AQUARIUS

Both signs value independence, freedom and open-mindedness. This makes for a harmonious and intellectually stimulating partnership. They share a passion for social causes, innovative ideas and a sense of adventure.

Overall creating a strong intellectual and emotional connection. Note that Sagittarius' bluntness may occasionally clash with Aquarius' desire for harmony and diplomacy.

SAGITTARIUS AND PISCES

Pisces' emotional depth and Sagittarius' optimism can create a unique and complementary connection. Pisces can provide emotional support and creativity. Sagittarius can bring excitement and new experiences into Pisces' life. Note that Sagittarius' need for independence may occasionally trigger Pisces' insecurities. With their positive traits and acknowledgement of challenges they can create harmony.

In conclusion, Sagittarius' love compatibility varies with each zodiac sign. Some signs offer a harmonious partnership based on shared values. Whilst others present challenges due to differing priorities. While compatibility is influenced by astrological factors, individual personalities and communication play a significant role in the success of a relationship. Ultimately, understanding and respecting each other's needs and differences are key to building a lasting and fulfilling connection for Sagittarius individuals.

TIPS FOR DATING AND MAINTAINING RELATIONSHIPS WITH SAGITTARIUS INDIVIDUALS

FOR MEN DATING SAGITTARIUS WOMEN

- **Embrace Adventure**: Sagittarius women are adventurous spirits. Plan exciting and spontaneous dates. Be open to trying new activities and exploring together.

- **Honesty is Key:** Sagittarius women appreciate honesty and direct communication. Be truthful and straightforward in your conversations.

- **Respect Independence**: Allow her the freedom she values. Don't try to restrict her or limit her personal space.

- **Share in Her Interests**: Show genuine interest in her passions and hobbies. Engage in conversations about travel, philosophy and intellectual topics.

- **Keep Things Fun**: Maintain a sense of humor and playfulness in your relationship. Make her laugh and enjoy lighthearted moments together.

- **Be Adventurous**: Surprise her with spontaneous getaways or outdoor adventures. She loves to explore new places and experiences.

- **Give Her Space**: Understand that Sagittarius women need independence and may sometimes require time alone. Respect her need for solitude without taking it personally.

- **Stay Positive:** Maintain a positive outlook on life, as Sagittarius women are attracted to optimism and enthusiasm.

- **Be Open-Minded**: Sagittarius men value intellectual curiosity and open-mindedness. Engage in stimulating conversations and explore new ideas together.

- **Join in the Adventure:** Embrace his love for adventure by participating in outdoor activities and spontaneous trips. Show that you can keep up with his zest for life.

- **Encourage Independence**: Allow him the freedom to pursue his interests and maintain his independence. Avoid being possessive or controlling.

- **Appreciate His Honesty**: Sagittarius men are known for their honesty. Value his candidness and be honest with him in return.

- **Laugh Together**: A sense of humor is essential in a relationship with a Sagittarius man. Share jokes and enjoy the lighter side of life.

- **Respect His Philosophical Side**: Sagittarius men often have a deep interest in philosophy and spirituality. Show respect for his beliefs and engage in meaningful conversations.

- **Support His Goals:** Encourage his ambitions and dreams. Be a supportive partner who helps him achieve his aspirations.

- **Give Him Space**: Understand that Sagittarius men need moments of solitude to recharge. Allow him the freedom to explore his interests independently.

Overall it's important to remember that astrological signs can give us some insights into people's personalities and preferences. However every individual is unique. No matter how compatible you may be astrologically, communication, respect and understanding are key in any relationship.

As we wrap up this chapter, it becomes apparent that Sagittarius' love life is an exhilarating journey filled with deep experiences. It's a realm where fiery passions, intellectual connections and deep emotions intertwine. Whether they're seeking love or already in a relationship, Sagittarius individuals can draw inspiration from their optimism and open heartedness.

Through their compatibility, with signs Sagittarius teaches us the value of embracing differences while still respecting each other's independence. They show us how to find joy in the journey of love. Although challenges may arise along the way these fiery archers possess the resilience and adaptability needed to navigate through the ups and downs of relationships.

As we come to the end of this chapter I hope you take with you the understanding of love and compatibility that Sagittarius represents. Lets celebrate the range of connections and embrace the endless possibilities, for exciting adventures in matters of the heart. Whether you're a Sagittarius looking for a partner or simply someone interested in astrology, may the stars always guide you on your journey to find love and happiness.

CHAPTER 3:
FRIENDS AND FAMILY

Welcome to the exciting world of Sagittarius when it comes to friendships and family relationships! Sagittarians are known for their enthusiasm, open mindedness and love for adventure. In this chapter we will take a journey through the qualities and dynamics that Sagittarius individuals bring to their friends and families. You're about to discover the challenges they face in relationships, the qualities that make them cherished friends and the dynamic interactions within their families. All of this and much more.

As we delve deeper into the world of Sagittarius you'll gain an understanding of how their adventurous spirit and zest for life shape their bonds with those they hold dear. Whether you're a Sagittarius seeking insight into your family connections or simply curious about astrology this chapter provides a comprehensive exploration of how Sagittarius functions as a friend, sibling, parent or child.

SAGITTARIUS AS A FRIEND

Having a friend who was born under the Sagittarius sign is like a breath of air in your life. They bring a combination of enthusiasm, spontaneity and optimism that can brighten the most mundane days. Let's take a closer look at what it's like to have a Sagittarius friend.

- **Adventurous**; Sagittarians are adventurers who are always up for trying new things and exploring different places. When you have a Sagittarius friend you can expect adventures and impromptu trips that will create happy memories.
- **Positive Vibes**; Sagittarius friends radiate positivity. Their infectious optimism can lift your spirits when you're feeling down. Their "glass half full" outlook on life is refreshing and comforting.
- **Open Mindedness**; Sagittarians are non judgmental individuals. They embrace people from all walks of life and are always eager to learn about other cultures or fresh perspectives. This makes them great friends for promoting inclusivity and diversity.
- **Honesty with Kindness**; Your Sagittarius friend will always tell you the truth as it is. They value

honesty and direct communication, which means they'll give you their opinion and advice with your interests, at heart.

- **Sense of Humor**; Sagittarians have a great sense of humor. They love to make others laugh. Having them around guarantees a fun filled time with plenty of moments and clever banter.

- **Independence**; Sagittarius friends highly value their independence much as they respect yours. They won't suffocate you with attention. Rest assured they'll be there for you whenever you need them.

- **Intellectual Stimulation**; Engaging in philosophical conversations is a delight for Sagittarians. They thrive on exploring ideas and sharing their perspectives on a range of topics. This makes them excellent companions for stimulating discussions.

- **Generosity**; Sagittarians are naturally generous. They are often the ones to extend a helping hand or offer support. They go out of their way to ensure that you feel valued and appreciated.

- **Restless Spirit**; While their adventurous nature is certainly appealing, Sagittarians may occasionally struggle with restlessness. They might alter plans. Make spur of the moment decisions, which can be both thrilling and challenging for their friends.

- **Unfiltered Honesty**; When it comes to honesty Sagittarius friends don't hold back. While this admirable quality should be appreciated it's important to brace yourself for their straightforwardness. Remember that they mean well.

In conclusion, having a Sagittarius friend translates into having an inspirational companion by your side, in life. Being around them is always enjoyable. Their adventurous nature guarantees that your friendship will be full of thrilling experiences. So cherish your Sagittarius friend because they bring a kind of enchantment into your life that cannot be replicated.

SAGITTARIUS AND FAMILY DYNAMICS

Sagittarius individuals bring a combination of optimism, enthusiasm and a spirit of adventure, to their families. Their approach to family life is characterized by a love for exploration, a thirst for knowledge and a strong sense of independence. Here's a close look at how Sagittarius interacts within the family;

- **The Adventurous Parent**; If you have a Sagittarius parent you're likely to experience someone who encourages exploration and adventure. They enjoy planning family vacations exposing you to cultures and instilling a love for learning and discovery.

- **The Optimistic Sibling**; Sagittarius siblings are known for their optimistic outlook on life. They bring joy and enthusiasm to family gatherings often becoming the life of the party. They are the ones who suggest road trips or outdoor adventures.

- **Independent Nature**; Sagittarius individuals value their independence within the context of family life. As such they may seek space and freedom to pursue their interests. This can sometimes lead them to be seen as the " spirit" in the family.

- **Honesty and Straightforwardness;** Sagittarians are recognized for being honest even, in a straightforward manner. During family discussions or conflicts they often express their opinions candidly while offering solutions.

- **Intellectual Stimulation**; Members of Sagittarius families thrive on intellectual stimulation. They delight in engaging in conversations, about philosophy and sharing their knowledge with others. When families come together it's not uncommon for debates and the exchange of ideas to take place.

- **Supportive**; Sagittarius individuals have a kind and caring nature. As such they are always there to support their family members. They willingly go the extra mile to lend a helping hand when loved ones are in need. They also are there to provide encouragement for them to pursue their dreams.

- **Respect for Differences**; Sagittarians are known for being open minded and accepting of others. They actively promote tolerance and inclusivity within their families. Often they take on the role of mediators during conflicts or disagreements.

- **Restlessness**; Every now and then Sagittarius family members may exhibit restlessness. They might seek out new experiences or crave change. This can bring excitement but it may also introduce some instability into the family dynamic.

- **Celebrating Traditions**; Despite their love for adventure Sagittarius individuals also value family traditions and gatherings. They understand the significance of connecting with loved ones during holidays and special occasions.

- **Role as Family Explorers**; It's quite common for Sagittarians to assume the role of being the family explorer. They often suggest trips or new hobbies to other family members. Furthermore they are likely to help with educational opportunities for younger siblings.

In conclusion, Sagittarius family members bring an element of adventure, optimism and intellectual curiosity into their households. They highly appreciate their freedom and the opportunity to explore. They also inspire their loved ones to embark on their quests of exploration. Although they can be straightforward and occasionally restless, their kindness, optimistic attitude and appreciation for diversity enhances the family dynamic.

CHALLENGES IN FRIENDSHIPS AND FAMILY RELATIONS

While Sagittarius individuals are widely recognized for their positive traits such as optimism, enthusiasm and a love for adventure they also encounter challenges. Being aware of these challenges can assist Sagittarians in navigating their relationships. Here are some things to be aware of.

- **Restlessness**; Sagittarians possess a desire for exploration and excitement. However this restlessness can occasionally result in a lack of commitment towards friendships or the tendency to constantly seek out experiences. It is crucial for Sagittarians to find a balance between their thirst for adventure and their responsibilities towards loved ones.

- **Bluntness and Honesty**; Known for their straightforwardness, this can inadvertently come across tactless or hurtful at times. Learning how to provide feedback with sensitivity is a challenge that they might need to overcome.

- **Independence**; Independence is highly cherished by Sagittarians. Although this may occasionally create the perception of distance or unavailability within relationships. Striking a balance between the need for space and nurturing intimate connections can prove challenging.

- **Commitment Issues;** It is not uncommon for Sagittarius individuals to be viewed as hesitant when it comes to commitments. Take time to reflect.

- **Hesitant**; One aspect of their nature is that they may jump into adventures without considering how it affects their loved ones leading to strain and misunderstandings. Additionally Sagittarians tend to resist routine and predictability which can pose challenges, in family life where routines often contribute to maintaining harmony.

- **Adventurous**; Another characteristic is their love for adventure, which could lead them to take risks that others perceive as irresponsible or dangerous. Striking a balance between their adventurous spirit and safety concerns becomes crucial in maintaining relationships.

- **Easily bored**; Sagittarians have a tendency to get easily bored which can affect their interactions with friends and family over time. Making an effort to stay engaged and committed in long term relationships is important.

- **Carefree**; When it comes to Sagittarians their carefree nature sometimes leads them to forget or overlook their responsibilities and commitments. This can be frustrating, for their friends and family members. Additionally Sagittarians often have a range of interests and hobbies which can make it difficult for them to effectively manage their time and energy.

To maintain fulfilling friendships and family relationships it's important for Sagittarius individuals to recognize and address these challenges. By embracing their qualities while also working on the pitfalls mentioned above Sagittarians can build strong and long lasting connections with their loved ones.

In the captivating realm of Sagittarius friendships and family dynamics we have uncovered a tapestry of qualities that make these individuals stand out. From their enthusiasm, to their love for adventure, Sagittarians bring a whirlwind of energy into the lives of those around them. Throughout this chapter we explored the challenges they face. Such as restlessness and straightforwardness. Along, with ways in which they can enhance and enrich their relationships. Within families Sagittarius members infuse curiosity and independence into the household dynamic. Among friends they light up circles with optimism and a great sense of humor.

As we bid farewell to this chapter I hope you carry with you an understanding of how Sagittarius fits within the context of friendships and family. If you're a Sagittarius looking to navigate the scene or someone trying to understand these individuals keep in mind that Sagittarius always seeks new adventures, connections and endless possibilities. May the essence of Sagittarius motivate you to embrace the world with open arms, cherish your loved ones and embark on thrilling journeys of exploration together. Life becomes an exhilarating voyage when you're surrounded by these archers.

CHAPTER 4:
CAREER AND MONEY

In this chapter we will embark on a journey through the ambitions, finances and unique qualities that define Sagittarius individuals as they strive for professional success. Sagittarians are known for their optimism, spirit and insatiable curiosity. As we delve deeper into the world of Sagittarius you will gain insights into how their adventurous nature and passion for learning shape their careers and finances.

Get ready to discover the Sagittarius perspective on career and money. Where optimism blends with exploration. Whether you are a Sagittarius looking to enhance your knowledge or someone interested in understanding the mindset of this vibrant sign this chapter will reveal the various aspects of how Sagittarius approaches wealth work and achieving goals.

CAREER PREFERENCES AND PROFESSIONAL ASPIRATIONS

Those born under the Sagittarius zodiac sign are widely recognized for their adventurous nature and enthusiastic demeanor. These characteristics significantly influence their career choices and professional aspirations. Let's dive deeper into the areas that Sagittarius individuals are naturally drawn to in their careers.

- **Travel and Adventure**; Sagittarians possess an affinity towards careers involving travel and adventure. Professions such as writers, photographers, tour guides or jobs within the travel and tourism industry. These vocations allow them to satiate their craving for exploring places and cultures.

- **Education and Intellectual Growth;** Sagittarius have an appreciation for knowledge acquisition and continuous learning. Many of them find fulfillment in roles as teachers or researchers. They derive satisfaction from sharing insights while inspiring others to broaden their perspectives through education.

- **Philosophy and Spiritual Exploration**; A number of Sagittarians display an interest in philosophical contemplation and spiritual pursuits. Some may pursue careers such as philosophers delving into life's questions or theologians studying faith based beliefs systems. Others may engage in practices related to astrology or metaphysics as they seek answers about life's purpose.

- **Media**; With natural communication skills, Sagittarius individuals often thrive in careers associated with media engagement. For example in journalism. Here they can share stories with a captivated audience.

- **Storytellers**; Sagittarius possesses a talent for storytelling. They captivate audiences with their infectious enthusiasm and natural charm.

- **Philanthropy**; Sagittarians often choose careers in charitable organizations, international aid agencies or fields that revolve around justice and humanitarian efforts.

- **Entrepreneurship;** Entrepreneurship appeals to Sagittarius individuals due to their adventurous side and love for freedom. Many of them embark on the journey of starting their own businesses in industries that align with their passions such as travel, education or adventure.

- **Competitive**; Sagittarians find fulfillment in sports and fitness due to their competitive spirits. They often excel as athletes, coaches or fitness trainers. Their unwavering dedication to challenges and personal growth propels them towards these pursuits.

- **Ethics**; Fields involving law and ethics hold an allure for Sagittarius individuals. They are naturally drawn to careers that involve fighting for justice and upholding principles. With a sense of justice they are willing to stand up for what they believe in.

- **Sales and marketing**; Sales and marketing roles suit Sagittarians thanks to their exceptional communication skills and persuasive abilities.

- **Healers**; Many Sagittarians have an interest in health, wellness and personal growth. They may choose to pursue careers as life coaches, therapists or healers helping others in their quest for self discovery.

Overall, Sagittarius individuals have diverse career interests due to a love for exploration and thirst for intellectual stimulation. They thrive in environments that allow them to be free spirited individuals who are always eager to learn. With their enthusiasm and optimism, Sagittarians ultimately bring a sense of adventure and positivity to any career path they embark on.

STRENGTHS THAT MAKE SAGITTARIUS INDIVIDUALS EXCEL IN THE WORKPLACE

Sagittarius individuals possess a unique set of strengths that leads to success in various professional settings. Their optimistic and adventurous nature, coupled with their passion for learning and exploration, make them valuable assets in the workplace. Here are some of the key strengths that help Sagittarius individuals to excel.

- **Optimism**: Sagittarians are natural optimists. Their positive outlook on life can inspire and motivate colleagues, even during challenging times. They tend to see opportunities in obstacles and approach problems with a "can-do" attitude, which can be infectious in the workplace.
- **Adaptability**: Sagittarius individuals thrive in dynamic environments. They easily adapt to change and are open to new ideas. This flexibility enables them to navigate shifting work landscapes and remain productive in ever-evolving industries.
- **Intellectual Depth**: Sagittarians have a profound thirst for knowledge and a love for intellectual exploration. They are constantly seeking to expand their horizons and delve into new subjects. This intellectual depth can lead to innovative solutions and fresh perspectives in the workplace.
- **Communication Skills**: Sagittarians are excellent communicators. They have a natural gift for storytelling and can convey ideas and information with enthusiasm and clarity. Their ability to articulate complex concepts makes them effective team members and leaders.
- **Team Player**: Despite their independent nature, Sagittarians work well within teams. They respect diverse perspectives and can foster collaboration by promoting an inclusive and open-minded work environment. Overall their optimism can also boost team morale.

- **Leadership Qualities:** Sagittarius individuals can make effective leaders due to their natural charisma and ability to inspire others. They are willing to take calculated risks and lead by example. Their passion and vision can motivate teams to achieve ambitious goals.

- **Global Perspective**: Sagittarians often have a global perspective and a deep appreciation for different cultures. This can be an asset in today's interconnected world, especially in industries with international reach or diverse clientele.

- **Problem-Solving Skills**: Their analytical thinking and problem-solving skills are enhanced by their love for intellectual challenges. Sagittarius individuals are resourceful and can find creative solutions to complex problems.

- **Resilience**: Sagittarians have a strong inner resilience that helps them bounce back from setbacks and failures. They don't dwell on past mistakes but view them as learning experiences, making them more resilient in the face of adversity.

- **Entrepreneurial Spirit:** Many Sagittarius individuals possess an entrepreneurial spirit. They thrive in roles that allow them to take risks and pursue their passions. Their independence and willingness to explore new opportunities make them well-suited for entrepreneurial endeavors.

- **Enthusiasm for Growth:** Sagittarians are constantly seeking personal and professional growth. They are proactive in pursuing opportunities for advancement and self-improvement, which can lead to career success.

In conclusion, Sagittarius individuals bring a unique blend of optimism, adaptability, intellectual curiosity and a global perspective to the workplace. Overall their strengths contribute to a positive work environment and often lead to success in a wide range of careers. From education and media to entrepreneurship and beyond.

CHALLENGES FACED BY SAGITTARIUS INDIVIDUALS IN THEIR CAREERS AND STRATEGIES TO OVERCOME THEM

While Sagittarius individuals possess numerous strengths that benefit them in the workplace, they also encounter certain challenges. Understanding these challenges and implementing effective strategies can help them navigate their careers more successfully. Here are some common career challenges faced by Sagittarius individuals and strategies to overcome them.

RESTLESSNESS AND IMPULSIVITY

- Challenge: Sagittarians can be restless and may struggle with the routine and stability that some careers demand. In addition their impulsivity can lead to hasty decisions.
- Strategy: Cultivate patience and discipline. Before making major career moves, thoroughly research and consider the potential consequences. Create a structured plan for achieving long-term goals.

COMMITMENT ISSUES

- Challenge: Sagittarius individuals may find it challenging to commit to long-term projects or roles. This can hinder career progression.
- Strategy: Focus on building skills and expertise in areas of genuine interest. Seek careers that allow for variety and exploration within a stable framework. Set achievable milestones to stay engaged.

TACTLESSNESS IN COMMUNICATION

- Challenge: Sagittarians' blunt and direct communication style may lead to misunderstandings or conflicts in the workplace.
- Strategy: Develop effective communication skills, including active listening and empathy. Learn to deliver feedback with sensitivity. Consider the perspectives of others before responding.

IMPATIENCE WITH HIERARCHIES

- Challenge: Sagittarians may become frustrated with hierarchical structures and rules in traditional workplaces.
- Strategy: Focus on the bigger picture and the opportunities for growth within the organization. Seek positions that allow for more autonomy and responsibility. Furthermore consider entrepreneurial ventures.

OVERCOMMITMENT AND BURNOUT

- Challenge: Sagittarius individuals' enthusiasm can lead them to overcommit to multiple projects, risking burnout.
- Strategy: Practice time management and prioritize tasks. Learn to say "no" when necessary and delegate responsibilities. Maintain a work-life balance to prevent exhaustion.

RESISTANCE TO ROUTINE

- Challenge: Sagittarians may struggle with repetitive tasks and routines.
- Strategy: Look for roles that offer a degree of variety and challenge. Seek positions that require problem-solving and creativity. Consider freelance or consulting work that allows for flexibility.

LACK OF ATTENTION TO DETAIL

- Challenge: Sagittarius individuals may overlook details while focusing on the big picture.
- Strategy: Develop organizational skills and use tools like checklists and calendars. Collaborate with colleagues who excel in attention to detail to complement your strengths.

IMPULSIVITY IN DECISION-MAKING

- Challenge: Sagittarians may make impulsive career decisions without fully considering the consequences.
- Strategy: Consult with trusted mentors or colleagues before making significant career choices. Take time to weigh pros and cons and assess potential risks.

SEEKING CONSTANT CHANGE

- Challenge: The desire for new experiences may lead to frequent job changes. This can hinder the development of long-term expertise.
- Strategy: Balance exploration with a commitment to mastery in chosen fields. Seek positions that encourage continuous learning and growth.

BALANCING INDEPENDENCE AND COLLABORATION

- Challenge: Sagittarians value independence but must also work effectively within teams.

- Strategy: Cultivate teamwork skills and find roles that allow for both independence and collaboration. Recognize that team efforts can lead to even more significant achievements.

By recognizing and addressing these obstacles, individuals born under the Sagittarius zodiac sign can make the most of their strengths while overcoming challenges in their lives. By employing strategies and being open to adaptation they can pursue successful career paths that align with their adventurous and optimistic nature.

In the captivating realm of Sagittarius professional and financial pursuits we have uncovered a tapestry woven with optimism, exploration and an insatiable thirst for knowledge. This chapter has taken us on a voyage through the strengths, obstacles and approaches that define Sagittarians as they strive for success and financial stability. As we bring this chapter to a close it becomes evident that Sagittarius individuals approach their careers and financial aspirations with a positive spirit and mindset. Their ability to embrace change along with their curiosity often leads them to diverse and fulfilling journeys. As they navigate the ups and downs of life they do so with resilience and optimism perceiving challenges as opportunities for growth.

May the insights gleaned from this chapter serve as a guiding light for Sagittarians who seek to accomplish their career goals. May it also provide understanding, for those who wish to appreciate the mindset of this zodiac sign. Best of luck to you all.

CHAPTER 5: SELF-IMPROVEMENT

Welcome to this chapter that delves into the world of self improvement as viewed through the lens of Sagittarius. Within these pages we will embark on a journey of growth, exploration and the pursuit of knowledge that is synonymous with Sagittarius individuals. Sagittarians possess a thirst for learning, a zest for life and an unwavering belief in the power of positivity. Throughout this chapter we will delve into how these remarkable qualities can be harnessed to cultivate self improvement and empower Sagittarians to realize their fullest potential.

Whether you are a Sagittarius seeking guidance on your path of growth or simply captivated by the distinctive mindset of this vibrant sign this chapter offers valuable insights, practical strategies and inspiration for embracing self improvement. So prepare to embark on a voyage of self discovery where each day presents an opportunity for learning and every challenge becomes a catalyst for growth. Let us follow the arrow of Archer as it guides us in our quest for self improvement.

PERSONAL GROWTH AND DEVELOPMENT FOR SAGITTARIUS

Sagittarius individuals are characterized by their adventurous spirit, optimism and love for exploration. They have a natural zest for life and a curiosity that drives them to seek new experiences and expand their horizons. While these qualities are their strengths, personal growth for Sagittarius often involves honing their boundless energy and enthusiasm into more focused and purposeful endeavors. Here are some key aspects of personal growth and development for Sagittarius individuals:

- **Embrace Commitment**: One of the key challenges for Sagittarians is their resistance to long-term commitments. Personal growth involves learning to commit to goals, relationships and projects that matter most. By cultivating commitment, they can see through their dreams to fruition and build lasting relationships.

- **Balance Freedom and Responsibility**: Sagittarius individuals treasure their independence. But personal growth requires finding a balance between the freedom they cherish and the responsibilities they must fulfill. Learning to navigate obligations without feeling confined is essential for their development.

- **Cultivate Patience**: Sagittarians can be impulsive and eager for instant results. Developing patience allows them to persevere through challenges and stay committed to long-term goals. Patience also helps them appreciate the journey as much as the destination.

- **Focus and Direction**: Their love for exploration can sometimes scatter their energy across various interests. Personal growth entails defining clear goals and channeling their enthusiasm into focused pursuits. Setting priorities and following through with dedication is key.

- **Embrace Routine**: Sagittarians often resist routine, but incorporating structure into their lives can help them achieve consistency and stability. Finding a healthy balance between spontaneity and routine is essential for personal growth.

- **Enhance Empathy**: Sagittarius individuals can be straightforward and blunt in their communication. Developing empathy and emotional intelligence allows them to connect more deeply with others. With this they can navigate relationships with greater sensitivity.

- **Harness Optimism**: While their optimism is a strength, personal growth involves using it to overcome challenges and setbacks. Sagittarians can learn to maintain their positivity while also being prepared for realistic assessments of situations.

- **Nurture Inner Wisdom**: Their love for knowledge often leads to a quest for wisdom. Personal growth entails not only acquiring knowledge but also cultivating inner wisdom through introspection, meditation and self-reflection.

- **Expand Cultural Awareness**: Sagittarius individuals' interest in different cultures and perspectives can be a source of personal growth. Engaging with diverse viewpoints and experiences enriches their understanding of the world . Ultimately it deepens their empathy.

- **Develop Financial Savvy**: Given their love for adventure, Sagittarians may benefit from enhancing their financial management skills. Learning about budgeting, saving and investing can provide them with the stability to pursue their passions.

- **Stay Grounded**: Personal growth involves finding ways to stay grounded amidst their adventurous pursuits. Practices like yoga, mindfulness, or spending time in nature can help Sagittarians maintain inner balance.

- **Seek Continuous Learning**: Sagittarius individuals thrive on learning. Personal growth involves a lifelong commitment to education and personal development. Pursuing new skills and knowledge keeps their curiosity alive.

In conclusion, personal growth and development for Sagittarius individuals involve striking a balance between their adventurous spirit and the need for focus. By harnessing their optimism, embracing responsibility and cultivating empathy, Sagittarians can continue their journey of self-discovery. A successful journey of exploration.

HARNESSING SAGITTARIUS STRENGTHS AND OVERCOMING WEAKNESSES

Sagittarius individuals possess a unique set of strengths and weaknesses, like every other zodiac sign. To maximize their potential and lead their best lives, Sagittarians can harness their strengths while actively working on overcoming their weaknesses. Here's how they can do that.

Strength: Optimism

- Harness: Embrace your natural optimism to inspire and uplift others. Your positivity can be a powerful force for motivation and resilience.

- Overcome: Be mindful of being overly optimistic in situations that require a more realistic assessment. Sometimes, acknowledging challenges is the first step in addressing them.

Strength: Curiosity and Learning

- Harness: Continue to explore new subjects and ideas. Your love for learning can lead to personal growth and career advancement.
- Overcome: Avoid spreading yourself too thin across multiple interests. Focus on mastering a few subjects or skills that align with your long-term goals.

Strength: Adventure and Exploration

- Harness: Embrace your adventurous spirit by seeking out new experiences and cultures. This can broaden your horizons and provide valuable life lessons.
- Overcome: Maintain a balance between adventure and stability. Recognize that some level of routine and commitment is necessary for personal and professional growth.

Strength: Honesty and Directness

- Harness: Use your honesty to build trust in your relationships. Your candidness can lead to open and transparent communication.
- Overcome: Practice delivering feedback with sensitivity, especially in delicate situations.

Consider the impact of your words on others' feelings.

Strength: Adaptability

- Harness: Leverage your adaptability to thrive in changing environments. Your ability to embrace new challenges can lead to career success.
- Overcome: Ensure that your adaptability doesn't result in a lack of commitment or follow-through. Set clear goals and stick to them.

Weakness: Impulsivity

Overcome: Pause and reflect before making major decisions. Develop a habit of considering the consequences of your actions to avoid hasty choices.

Weakness: Resistance to Routine

Overcome: Introduce structured routines into your life, especially in areas that require consistency. For example, health and finance. Balance spontaneity with stability.

Weakness: Commitment Issues

Overcome: Recognize the value of commitment in achieving long-term goals. Set achievable milestones and focus on building lasting relationships.

Weakness: Tactlessness

Overcome: Practice empathy and active listening to understand others' perspectives. Think before speaking, especially in sensitive or emotional situations.

Weakness: Restlessness

Overcome: Channel your restlessness into productive outlets. Set clear goals and create a structured plan to avoid constant changes and distractions.

Weakness: Lack of Attention to Detail

Overcome: Use organizational tools and techniques to help you stay on top of details. Collaborate with detail-oriented individuals in projects where precision is crucial.

Weakness: Overcommitment

Overcome: Learn to say "no" when necessary and prioritize your commitments. Focus on quality rather than quantity in your projects and relationships.

By acknowledging their strengths and actively addressing their weaknesses, individuals born under the Sagittarius zodiac sign can lead more well rounded and satisfying lives. Embracing their love for adventure while cultivating discipline and dedication will enable them to harness their qualities and overcome obstacles effectively.

As we wrap up this chapter on self improvement in relation to Sagittarius where we have explored the characteristics and qualities that define this sign known for its nature and optimistic outlook. Overall Sagittarians possess the tools to make significant progress in their pursuit of self improvement. By embracing their strengths while addressing challenges head on they can soar to new heights in many areas of life.

May the essence of Sagittarius ignite your drive to forge your journey, towards personal growth. A journey where passion and knowledge intertwine. Let every obstacle become a milestone on the path to a richer and more satisfying existence.

<h1 style="text-align:center">CHAPTER 6:
THE YEAR AHEAD</h1>

Welcome to this chapter that delves into the outlook for Sagittarius in the year ahead. In this chapter we will explore how celestial events and astrological alignments might shape the lives of individuals born under the sign of Sagittarius.

As a Sagittarian you possess a sense of optimism, curiosity and a thirst for adventure on your life's journey. Over the upcoming year the movements of stars and planets will impact your professional experiences. This chapter aims to provide insights into what lies ahead and how you can make the most of opportunities while navigating any challenges that may arise.

So get ready, Sagittarian! Prepare to embark on a voyage where optimism intertwines with introspection. Let the Archers arrow guide you towards a year of growth, adventure and self discovery.

HOROSCOPE GUIDE FOR THE YEAR AHEAD

CAREER AND FINANCES

This year promises shifts in your career. Your limitless enthusiasm and adaptability will help you overcome obstacles while seizing opportunities. Keep an eye out for advancement opportunities. Remember the importance of balancing your adventurous spirit with financial stability. It would be wise to make well informed investment decisions that will secure your future.

Sagittarius individuals have a lot of potential in their careers and financial situations this year. Here are some astrological events that will play a role in shaping these aspects of your life.

- **Jupiter in Pisces (May. October);** During Jupiter's transit through Pisces you may experience a sense of creativity and intuition when it comes to your career. It's a time to explore new opportunities or projects that align with your passions. Financially this period is favorable for investments and expanding your sources of income.

- **Saturn in Aquarius (Throughout the Year);** Saturn's influence continues to impact your career sector as it moves through Aquarius. This urges you to establish long term goals and pursue them diligently. You might find yourself taking on new responsibilities at work which can lead to career advancement and financial stability.

- **Solar and Lunar Eclipses;** Keep an eye out for changes in your situation during the eclipse in Taurus (April 30) and lunar eclipse, in Taurus (November 8). These celestial events could bring about shifts or developments. Please exercise caution when making investments and financial decisions during these periods and take the time to reassess your budget.

- **Mars in Aries; Between January 6th and March 3rd Mars**, Mars in Aries can provide a boost of energy and motivation to propel your career forward. Utilize this time to take initiative and pursue your goals with enthusiasm.

Overall to maximize your career and financial prospects, Sagittarius it is important to set goals, maintain discipline in your pursuits and explore new opportunities. Be mindful of choices during eclipse periods. Lastly, consider seeking professional advice when needed.

LOVE AND RELATIONSHIPS

Sagittarians can expect love to be in the air this year. If you're already in a relationship your bond will deepen as you continue to communicate honestly with your partner. For those who're single, keep an open heart for new connections as someone special may unexpectedly enter your life.

Your relationships will flourish throughout the year Sagittarius. Your honesty and direct communication will strengthen your connections with loved ones. Be open to forming friendships and deepening existing ones. Singles might find new love so again it's important to keep an open heart.

In the year ahead, Sagittarius individuals should anticipate their love lives and relationships being influenced by significant astrological events. These celestial movements may bring both challenges and chances for matters of the heart.

- **Jupiter transits through Pisces;** During the period from May to October with Jupiter transiting through Pisces, which happens to be your ruling planet. You can expect enhancements in your emotional world. You might experience a connection to your instincts and emotions which can deepen your relationships. It's a time to nurture the bonds you already have and explore the depths of your emotions.
- **Saturn in Aquarius (Throughout the Year);** With Saturn remaining in Aquarius it encourages you to assess the dynamics of your connections, including friendships and romantic relationships. You may find yourself desiring genuine connections in your love life. It's a period of growth and maturity within your relationships.
- **Solar and Lunar Eclipses;** The solar eclipse in Taurus (April 30) and lunar eclipse in Taurus

(November 8) could bring about changes and revelations in your partnerships. These eclipses might lead you to reevaluate what you value in relationships and let go of any attachments that no longer contribute positively to your well being.

- **Venus in Sagittarius (December 30. January 23 2024);** When Venus graces Sagittarius it enhances your charisma and attractiveness. This is a time for Sagittarians to shine when it comes to love and romance. Embrace this opportunity to openly express your feelings and attract attention.

Overall focus on strengthening connections, nurturing existing relationships and seeking authenticity, within all of your interactions. Stay receptive to the changes that eclipses may bring. Remember they often lead to growth and development in your emotional world.

PERSONAL GROWTH

Sagittarius this year beckons you to tap into your wisdom, explore your passions and seize opportunities for growth. Harness the energies of astrology to embark on a journey of self discovery and improvement. With your optimism and adventurous spirit you hold massive potential for profound personal development throughout this year. Here are some key astrological events of the year that present you with opportunities for growth and self discovery.

- **Jupiters journey through Pisces (May. October);** During this period take the time to delve into your world and embrace your intuition.

Engaging in spiritual practices, creative endeavors or deep introspection can help foster growth.

- **Saturn's presence in Aquarius (Throughout the Year);** Saturn's influence encourages self reflection and personal development. Utilize this time to identify areas for improvement and focus on nurturing yourself.
- **Solar and Lunar Eclipses;** Eclipses have the potential to spark revelations. Embrace the changes and insights they bring as they often pave the way for growth and self discovery.

HEALTH AND WELLBEING

Sagittarius folks should focus on their health and overall well being in the year as astrological happenings can have an impact on your energy levels.

- **Jupiter in Pisces (May. October);** When Jupiter moves through Pisces it can enhance your creative endeavors. However it's important to maintain an approach to your well being. Embrace mindfulness practices to nurture your emotional fitness.
- **Saturn in Aquarius (Throughout the Year);** With Saturn in Aquarius you may find yourself inclined towards health routines. Consider incorporating exercise into your routine and prioritize your well being.
- **Solar and Lunar Eclipses;** Eclipses tend to heighten sensitivity. During these times pay attention to your health. Seek support from friends or professionals if needed.

Overall to ensure a healthy body and mind Sagittarius individuals should give importance to exercise, mental wellness practices and emotional balance. Balancing with self care routines will help you maintain vitality throughout the year.

TRAVEL AND ADVENTURE

As an adventurer at heart within the zodiac realm this year presents perfect opportunities to explore new horizons. Plan trips ahead of time while also embracing spontaneous adventures along the way.

FAMILY RELATIONSHIPS

This year your bond with family members will be strong. Make sure to spend quality time and engage in deep conversations. Your positive outlook can uplift your loved ones when they face challenges.

CREATIVITY AND HOBBIES

Get ready for a surge of creativity in the year ahead. Pursue projects that ignite your passions. Your enthusiasm and inspiration will lead to creating something magnificent.

SOCIAL LIFE

Your social calendar is going to be quite busy, Sagittarius! Embrace opportunities to meet people and expand your network. Your charm and charisma will make you a popular figure in diverse social circles.

SPIRITUALITY AND INNER HARMONY

Consider nurturing your spiritual side this year. Explore spiritual practices such as in meditation or taking time for self reflection. Connecting with your inner self will bring you a sense of peace and purpose.

CHALLENGES

While the year ahead holds promise for you it's important to be mindful of impulsiveness and impatience. Avoid making hasty decisions especially when it comes to financial matters. Remember to strike a balance between your thirst for adventure and your responsibilities.

Overall the year ahead is full of potential, for growth both personally and professionally. Embrace the chances that come your path, remain faithful to your outlook. Utilize your limitless passion to craft a life brimming with excitement and satisfaction. Revel in the voyage!

Astrological events play a significant role in influencing the lives of individuals, and Sagittarius is no exception. As a Sagittarius, you are ruled by Jupiter, the planet of expansion and optimism. Here are some key astrological events to watch out for in the coming year and their potential impact on your life:

- **Jupiter Transits;** Jupiter in Pisces (May - October): During this period, Jupiter, your ruling planet, moves through the compassionate and intuitive sign of Pisces. This alignment can enhance your spiritual and creative pursuits. You may feel a stronger urge to explore your inner world, engage in artistic endeavors, or deepen your spiritual practices. It's a time for personal growth and introspection.

- **Saturn Transits;** Saturn in Aquarius (Throughout the Year): Saturn continues its transit through Aquarius, which can bring a sense of responsibility and discipline to your social life and friendships. You may find yourself reevaluating your social circles and focusing on building more meaningful connections. It's a time for aligning your personal values with your social interactions.

- **Lunar and Solar Eclipses;** Solar Eclipse in Taurus (April 30): This eclipse may highlight financial matters for you, Sagittarius. It's a good time to review your financial goals, investments, and budgeting habits.

- **Lunar Eclipse in Taurus (November 8):** Another eclipse in Taurus emphasizes your values and possessions. It's an opportunity to let go of what no longer serves you and make changes in your material life.
- **Mercury Retrogrades;** Mercury Retrograde in Air Signs (January 14 - February 3, May 10 - June 3, and September 9 - October 2): During these retrogrades, communication may become more challenging. Be cautious with contracts and agreements. It's a time for reevaluating your communication style and ensuring clarity in important conversations.
- **Mars Transits;** Mars in Aries (January 6 - March 3): Mars in Aries can bring an extra boost of energy and motivation. You may feel more assertive in pursuing your goals and ambitions. Use this period to initiate projects and take calculated risks.
- **Venus Transits;** Venus in Sagittarius (December 30 - January 23, 2024): When Venus enters your sign, it brings a harmonious and social energy. It's a great time to enhance your personal charm and enjoy social interactions. Your optimism and charisma will shine.

Remember that while astrological events can provide insights into potential themes and energies, how they manifest in your life depends on your individual birth chart. Use these influences as opportunities for personal growth, self-reflection, and positive change. Embrace the adventurous and optimistic spirit of Sagittarius as you navigate the celestial events in the year ahead.

As we wrap up this chapter we've explored the path that awaits individuals born under the sign of Sagittarius, in the year. From matters of the heart to ambitions. From health and wellness to personal development. The stars and planets have revealed a tapestry of opportunities and challenges.

Sagittarius, your natural optimism, endless curiosity and adventurous nature will serve as your guiding principles as you navigate the influences of the year ahead. Embrace the lessons that come your way remembering that every challenge presents an opportunity for growth and every adventure offers a chance for self discovery.

As you traverse through the year, always keep in mind that an archer's arrow points towards a future filled with promise and excitement. Whether you're exploring new horizons or delving into the depths of your soul may this upcoming year be a time of personal growth, fulfillment and realization of your most ambitious aspirations.

CHAPTER 7:
FAMOUS "SAGITTARIUS" PERSONALITIES

In this chapter we'll take a dive into the lives of some known individuals who were born under the Sagittarius zodiac sign. These remarkable people have left an impact in various fields of human achievement. Sagittarius folks are renowned for their nature, inquisitive minds and boundless curiosity. It comes as no surprise that many accomplished individuals share this sign.

As we explore the journeys and achievements of these Sagittarians we'll discover a tapestry of talent spanning politics, entertainment, sports and much more. Each profile will unveil the qualities that make Sagittarius individuals stand out from the crowd – from their pursuit of goals to their charismatic and outspoken personalities.

Embark on this journey, through the lives of Sagittarius personalities as we delve into the driving forces that have propelled them towards greatness. Their stories serve as a source of inspiration. Their legacies continue to shape our world in ways.

WINSTON CHURCHILL

- Date of Birth: November 30, 1874.
- Brief Biography: Sir Winston Churchill was a British statesman, army officer, and writer. He is best known for his leadership as Prime Minister of

the United Kingdom during World War II. Churchill's speeches and determination inspired the British people during the darkest hours of the war.

- Sagittarius Traits: Adventurous, optimistic, charismatic, direct and outspoken.

- Impact: Churchill's leadership and unwavering resolve played a pivotal role in the Allied victory in World War II. His speeches, such as the famous "We shall fight on the beaches", continue to be celebrated for their inspiration.

- Personal Life: Churchill was a prolific writer, earning the Nobel Prize in Literature in 1953. He had a lifelong love of adventure, painting and travel.

CATHY MORIARTY

- Date of Birth: November 29, 1960.
- Brief Biography: Cathy Moriarty is an American actress best known for her role as Vicki LaMotta in the film "Raging Bull" (1980), for which she received an Academy Award nomination.
- Sagittarius Traits: Energetic, optimistic, outgoing and adventurous.
- Impact: Moriarty's performance in "Raging Bull" earned her critical acclaim and recognition in the film industry. She has continued to work in film and television, showcasing her versatile talent.
- Personal Life: Moriarty's career has spanned several decades. She remains an influential figure in Hollywood.

BRUCE LEE

- Date of Birth: November 27, 1940.
- Brief Biography: Bruce Lee was a martial artist, actor and filmmaker known for his groundbreaking contributions to martial arts and action cinema. He is considered one of the most influential martial artists of all time.
- Sagittarius Traits: Determined, adventurous, focused and enthusiastic.
- Impact: Bruce Lee's martial arts philosophy and innovative techniques revolutionized martial arts and popularized it worldwide. His films, such as "Enter the Dragon," left an indelible mark on cinema.

- Personal Life: Beyond his martial arts prowess, Lee was a philosopher and author. His legacy continues to inspire generations of martial artists and actors.

TAYLOR SWIFT

- Date of Birth: December 13, 1989.
- Brief Biography: Taylor Swift is an American singer-songwriter and actress. She is known for her narrative songwriting and has won numerous awards, including multiple Grammy Awards.
- Sagittarius Traits: Creative, optimistic, independent and charismatic.
- Impact: Swift's music has resonated with millions worldwide, making her one of the most successful and influential contemporary artists. Her albums have topped charts and earned critical acclaim.
- Personal Life: Swift is also known for her philanthropic efforts and advocacy on various social and political issues.

NICKI MINAJ

- Date of Birth: December 8, 1982.
- Brief Biography: Nicki Minaj is a Trinidadian-American rapper, singer, and songwriter. She is known for her bold and theatrical persona and has achieved significant success in the music industry.
- Sagittarius Traits: Outspoken, confident, ambitious and adventurous.

- Impact: Minaj's music has garnered millions of fans worldwide. Also she has been recognized for her contributions to hip-hop and pop culture.
- Personal Life: Beyond her music career, Minaj has ventured into acting and philanthropy. She is recognized as a multifaceted and influential artist.

FRANZ FERDINAND

- Date of Birth: December 18, 1863.
- Brief Biography: Archduke Franz Ferdinand of Austria was a royal figure whose assassination in 1914 triggered the events leading to World War I.
- Sagittarius Traits: Adventurous, determined and driven by principles.
- Impact: The assassination of Franz Ferdinand set in motion a series of events that ultimately led to World War I, reshaping the course of history.
- Personal Life: Beyond his historical role, Franz Ferdinand was known for his love of hunting and his progressive ideas. This included advocating for greater autonomy within the Austro-Hungarian Empire.

EMMANUEL MACRON

- Date of Birth: December 21, 1977.
- Brief Biography: Emmanuel Macron is a French politician who became the President of France in 2017. He is known for his centrist policies and youthful approach to governance.

- Sagittarius Traits: Charismatic, visionary and open-minded.

- Impact: Macron's election as President marked a significant shift in French politics. He has been a prominent figure in European and international politics.

- Personal Life: Macron's rise to power at a relatively young age reflects his ambitious and adventurous spirit.

IAN BOTHAM

- Date of Birth: November 24, 1955.

- Brief Biography: Sir Ian Botham is a former English cricketer and one of the greatest all-rounders in the history of cricket. He achieved numerous records during his career.

- Sagittarius Traits: Competitive, energetic, adventurous and determined.
- Impact: Botham's cricketing prowess made him a legendary figure in the sport. He contributed significantly to England's cricket success during his era.
- Personal Life: Botham's love for adventure extended beyond the cricket field, as he embarked on charity walks and humanitarian efforts.

SINEAD O'CONNOR

- Date of Birth: December 8, 1966.
- Brief Biography: Sinead O'Connor was an Irish singer-songwriter known for her distinctive voice and socially conscious lyrics. She gained international fame with her hit song "Nothing Compares 2 U."
- Sagittarius Traits: Bold, outspoken and driven by principles.
- Impact: O'Connor's music and activism have resonated with audiences worldwide. She was celebrated for her fearless approach to art and social justice.
- Personal Life: O'Connor's career has been marked by both artistic achievements and personal challenges. She was a complex and influential figure.

SCARLETT JOHANSSON

- Date of Birth: November 22, 1984.

- Brief Biography: Scarlett Johansson is an American actress and singer known for her versatile roles in film. She has received critical acclaim and numerous awards throughout her career.
- Sagittarius Traits: Adventurous, confident and charismatic.
- Impact: Johansson's acting talent has made her one of the most sought-after and highest-paid actresses in Hollywood. Her performances have left a lasting impact on cinema.
- Personal Life: Beyond her acting career, Johansson has ventured into music and has been an advocate for various social and humanitarian causes.

LARRY BIRD

- Date of Birth: December 7, 1956.
- Brief Biography: Larry Bird is a former American professional basketball player and coach. He is widely regarded as one of the greatest basketball players in history.
- Sagittarius Traits: Competitive, determined and driven by a love for the game.
- Impact: Bird's contributions to basketball include multiple NBA championships and MVP awards. He has left an indelible mark on the sport.
- Personal Life: Bird's dedication to basketball extended beyond his playing career. He went on to become a successful coach and executive in the NBA.

KAREN GILLAN

- Date of Birth: November 28, 1987.
- Brief Biography: Karen Gillan is a Scottish actress known for her roles in television and film. She gained prominence for her role as Amy Pond in the TV series "Doctor Who."
- Sagittarius Traits: Energetic, outgoing and adventurous.
- Impact: Gillan's talent and versatility as an actress have earned her acclaim in both British and international entertainment. She has continued to excel in her career.
- Personal Life: Gillan's journey in the entertainment industry reflects her adventurous and determined spirit, as she has transitioned from acting to directing.

These profiles showcase the talents and achievements of known individuals who were born under the Sagittarius sign. Whether in politics, entertainment, sports or art Sagittarius individuals have made a significant impact on the world.

As we conclude this chapter dedicated to Sagittarius personalities we have embarked on a captivating journey through the lives and accomplishments of those who share this zodiac sign. Their stories span domains like politics, entertainment, sports and beyond. Their journeys serve as evidence of the potential and determination that define Sagittarius. Their fearlessness, in pursuing dreams, eagerness to explore territories and commitment to their beliefs are just a few of the qualities that have propelled them towards greatness.

Let us celebrate these Sagittarius personalities' legacies and allow their stories to inspire us on our paths. Whether you belong to this zodiac sign or simply admire the attributes it embodies, always remember that the essence of Sagittarius lives on in the souls of those who dare to dream, discover and leave a lasting imprint on the world.

CONCLUSION

As we approach the culmination of our journey through the world of Sagittarius, it's time to reflect on the key insights and wisdom we've gained about this dynamic zodiac sign. In this concluding chapter, we'll summarize the essential points we've explored in each of the preceding chapters.

Summarization of Key Points about Sagittarius:

- **Chapter 1 - History and Mythology**: In this chapter we explored the historical and mythological origins of Sagittarius. We discovered how different cultures perceived and represented the Archer in their star maps. Furthermore we traced the evolution of Sagittarius from mythological interpretations to modern astrology.

- **Chapter 2 - Love & Compatibility**: In this chapter we delved into Sagittarius' approach to love and romance. Inside we analyzed Sagittarius' compatibility with other zodiac signs. Lastly we offered tips for dating and maintaining relationships with Sagittarius individuals.

- **Chapter 3 - Friends And Family**: Here we explored Sagittarius' role as a friend and family member. Inside we discussed the dynamics and challenges in friendships and family relations for Sagittarius.

- **Chapter 4 - Career And Money**: This chapter explored Sagittarius' career preferences and professional aspirations. It highlighted the strengths that make Sagittarius individuals excel in the workplace. It also addressed the challenges Sagittarius individuals may face in their careers and provided strategies to overcome them.

- **Chapter 5 - Self-Improvement**: In this chapter we explored personal growth and development for Sagittarius. We discussed how to harness Sagittarius' strengths and overcome weaknesses. Furthermore we offered exercises and outlooks for potential self-improvement.

- **Chapter 6 - The Year Ahead**: In this chapter we Analyzed how astrological events of the year influence Sagittarius individuals. We looked in detail at the way it influenced love, career, health, personal growth and much more.

- **Chapter 7 - Famous "Sagittarius" Personalities:** Here we were introduced to profiles of famous individuals born under the Sagittarius sign. Inside we explored their impact and the traits that define them.

As we near the conclusion of our exploration of Sagittarius it's crucial to bear in mind that the essence of the Archer is characterized by a nature unwavering positivity and an insatiable search for truth and adventure. These qualities do not only define individuals born under Sagittarius. They also have a profound impact on the world. May the wisdom and understanding you have acquired about Sagittarius inspire you to embrace these attributes throughout your journey and appreciate the spirit embodied by this zodiac sign.

Throughout this book we embarked on a captivating voyage to unravel the nature of Sagittarius. Our objective was to offer insights, guidance and a deeper understanding of what it means to be a Sagittarius. We explored many aspects such as its history, mythical origins and astrological significance. We delved into topics like love, relationships, friendships, family dynamics, career aspirations, personal growth and more. Cosmic influences will influence Sagittarius individuals in the upcoming year. Furthermore we celebrated personalities who share this zodiac sign while aiming to empower all Sagittarius individuals to embrace their qualities fully.

Our mission in this book was centered around helping a Sagittarius unlock their full potential while navigating life's adventures, with confidence and authenticity. We have fulfilled our promise by providing an exploration of Sagittarius offering insights and unveiling the dynamic characteristics that define this zodiac sign. From delving into the ancient origins to offering guidance on matters of love, career and personal development our aim was to equip Sagittarius individuals with the knowledge and resources they need to flourish.

If there's one major lesson to be gleaned from this book it is the celebration of Sagittarius' distinct qualities; their curiosity, unwavering optimism, adventurous spirit and fearless pursuit of truth and excitement. These qualities are not only attributes; they epitomize what it means to be a Sagittarius. Our hope is that every Sagittarius reader who engages with this book will develop an appreciation for their strengths and experience a renewed sense of purpose in embracing life's adventures.

In conclusion astrology serves as a tool for self discovery and personal growth due to its insights into human nature and cosmic influences. The representation of the Archer as the symbol for the Sagittarius zodiac sign reminds us of the power of optimism, the thrill of exploration and the significance of embracing our qualities.

As we navigate through the changing universe we want to inspire all Sagittarius individuals to embrace their strengths, overcome challenges and keep aiming for a better future. Dear Sagittarius you embody endless possibilities and boundless optimism. Your adventurous nature knows no limits and your unwavering quest for truth and purpose is truly inspiring. Embrace your qualities with pride as they serve as your guiding compass on this journey. As you explore the horizons of life remember that even the stars themselves celebrate your spirit.

This book has been a tribute to the nature and celebration of everything that makes Sagittarius special. As we bring this journey to an end our hope is that you will carry a better understanding of your sign, an increased appreciation for your strengths and be inspired to face life's adventures with unwavering optimism. Whether you are a Sagittarius or someone seeking insight into this sign may the wisdom within these pages light up your path and lead you towards a future filled with exploration, discovery and limitless enthusiasm. Best wishes!